ŠEVČÍK

OPUS 8

CHANGES OF POSITION &
PREPARATORY SCALE STUDIES

LAGENWECHSEL UND
TONLEITERVORSTUDIEN

CHANGEMENT DE POSITIONS
ET EXERCICES PRÉPARATOIRES
DE GAMMES

FOR

CELLO

ARR. H. BOYD

BOSWORTH

Preface

The adapting of Professor O. Ševčik's Violin Exercises (Op. 8) for the Violoncello, has been undertaken in the hope that they will be of great service to students in the mastery of the difficulties of "shifting." We believe that these Exercises form a scheme of detailed practice of "Positions," that has not before been included in Violoncello Technical Studies. The Bowings are as in the original, but it should be remembered that to obtain the greatest benefit from these Exercises, they should be practised with a variety of bowings. For this purpose the Ševčik-Feuillard Bowing Technique, Op. 2. Part I would be invaluable.

Haidee Boyd (Pupil of Professor J. Klengel, Leipsic)
Helen Boyd (Pupil of Professor O. Ševčik, Prague)

Préface

L'arrangement pour violoncelle de „ Changements de positions et exercices préparatoires de gammes" par O. Sevcik, Op. 8 (édité jusqu'à présent pour violon) a été fait en vue d'aider les élèves de surmonter les difficultés des changements de positions et déplacements des doigts. Nous faisons ressortir que ces études, pour en retirer toute l'utilité, doivent être jouées autant que possible avec différents coups d'archet. A cet effet, la „Technique de l'archet pour violoncelle par Sevcik-Feuillard" Op. 2 partie I est indispensable.

Haidee Boyd (élève du prof. J. Klengel à Leipzig)
Helen Boyd (élève du prof. O. Sevcik à Prague)

Vorwort

Die Bearbeitung der Lagenwechsel und Tonleiter-Vorstudien von O. Sevcik, Op. 8 (bisher nur erschienen für Violine) für das Violoncello ist in der Hoffnung unternommen worden, daß sie Schülern behilflich sein werden, die Schwierigkeiten bei Lagenwechsel und Rückungen zu überwinden. Wir bemerken hierzu noch, daß diese Studien, um den richtigen Nutzen davon zu haben, möglichst in verschiedenen Stricharten gespielt werden müssen. Zu diesem Zwecke ist die Bogentechnik für Violoncello von Sevcik-Feuillard Op. 2 Teil I unentbehrlich.

Haidee Boyd (Schülerin von Prof. J. Klengel, Leipzig)
Helen Boyd (Schülerin von Prof. O. Sevcik, Prag)

Předmluva

Přikročujíce ku vydání přepracovaného Ševčíkova díla Op. 8: „Změny poloh a průprava ke cvičení stupnic," jež byly dosud pouze pro housle, také pro violoncello, činíme tak v umyslu, abychom pomohli žákům překonati obtíže vyskytující se při změnách a přesunech poloh. Připomínáme, že tyto studie jest nutno hráti různými smyky, mají-li přinésti žádoucí užitek. K tomuto cíli jest nevyhnutelnou „Škola smyčcové techniky" od Ševčíka-Feuillarda Op. 2 část I.

Haidee Boyd (Žačka prof. J. Klengela v Lipsku)
Helen Boyd (Žačka prof. O. Ševčíka v Praze)

B. & Cº 18488

Changes of position

Practice these examples in moderato tempo:
a) each bar separately,
b) each bar with the next-following one, thus: 1 to 2, 2 to 8, 8 to 4, etc.
c) all the bars shown to lie on the same string, thus: in the 1st example bars 1 to 5, 6 to 10, 11 to 15, 16 to 21,
d) the whole example in the following keys both legato and detached.

Lagenwechselübungen

Bei dem Einüben dieser Beispiele wiederhole man in gemäßigtem Tempo:
a) jeden einzelnen Takt,
b) jeden Takt mit dem nächstfolgenden (1-2, 2-8, 8-4, u. s. w.),
c) alle Takte, die auf derselben Saite angezeigt sind (im 1ten Beispiele Takte 1-5, 6-10, 11-15, 16-21,),
d) das ganze Beispiel in folgenden Tonarten, gebunden und gestoßen:

Changement de positions

En exerçant ces exemples il faut répéter dans le mouvement modére:
a) chaque mesure séparément,
b) chaque mesure avec la suivante (1-2, 2-8, 8-4 etc.),
c) toutes les mesures, qui sont indiquées sur la même corde (dans le 1er exemple les mesures 1-5, 6-10, 11-15, 16-21,)
d) tout l'exemple dans les tons suivants, en lié et en détaché:

Cvičení ve výměně poloh

Při cvičené těchto příkladů jest nut no opakovati ve volném pohybu:
a) každý, jednotlivý takt,
b) každý takt s následujícím 1-2, 2-8, 8-4, atd.),
c) všecky takty označené na téže struně (v 1. příkladu takty 1-5, 6-10, 11-15, 16-21,),
d) celý příklad v následujících toninách, vázaně i odráženě:

In the following exercises the position of the fingers is only shown in C major. In playing these in other keys care must be taken to use correct fingering.

In den folgenden Übungen ist die Fingerstellung nur von C-dur angegeben. Beim Spielen derselben in anderen Tonarten muß auf richtigen Fingersatz geachtet werden.

La position des doigts dans les exercices suivants est celle en Ut majeur. Il y a lieu de veiller au doigter exact lors de leur exécution dans d'autres tonalités.

V následujících cvičeních jest uveden prstoklad jen v tonině C dur. Hrají-li se tato cvičeni v jiných stupnicích, je třeba dbáti správného prstokladu.

1

Changes of position:
from 1st to 2nd, 2nd to 3rd, 3rd to 4th, etc.
Wechsel der Lagen:
1-2, 2-3, 3-4, u. s. w.

Changement des positions:
1-2, 2-3, 3-4, etc.
Výměna poloh:
1-2, 2-3, 3-4, atd.

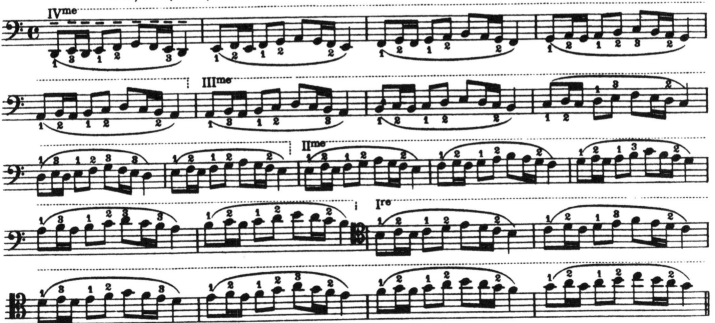

B. & Co 18488

4

2.

3.

4.

5.

6.

7.

8.

Changes of position:	Changement des positions:
from 1st to 3rd, 2nd to 4th, 3rd to 5th etc.	1-3, 2-4, 3-5 etc.
Wechsel der Lagen:	**Vymena poloh:**
1-3, 2-4, 3-5 u.s.w.	1-3, 2-4, 3-5 atd.

9.

10.

11.

12.

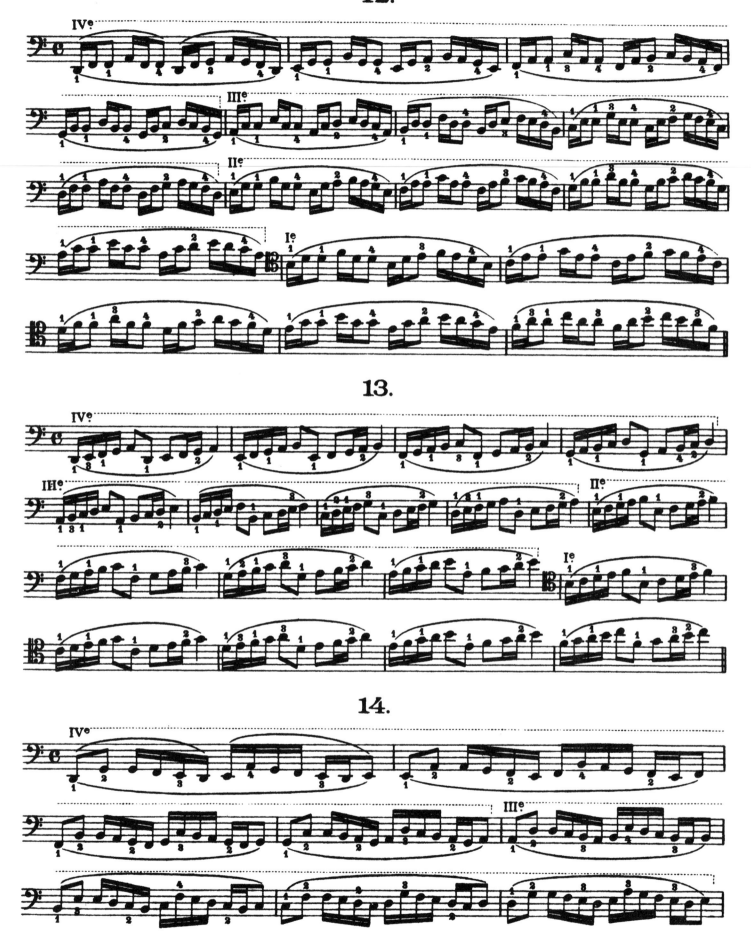

13.

14.

15.

16.

Changes of position:	Changement des positions:
from 1st to 4th, 2nd to 5th, 3rd to 6th etc.	1-4, 2-5, 3-6 etc.
Wechsel der Lagen:	**Výměna poloh:**
1-4, 2-5, 3-6 u.s.w.	1-4, 2-5, 3-6 atd.

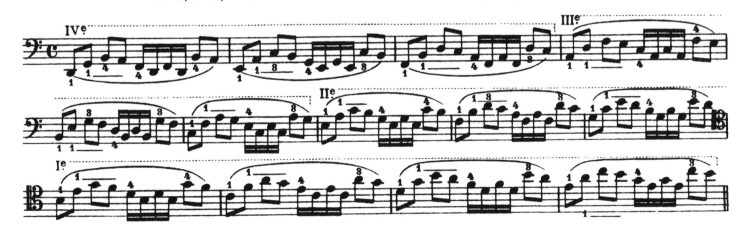

17.

18.

19.

20.

21.

22.

23.

Changes of position:
from 1st to 5th, 2nd to 6th, 3rd to 7th etc.

Wechsel der Lagen:
1 - 5, 2 - 6, 3 - 7 u.s.w.

Changement des positions:
1 - 5, 2 - 6, 3 - 7 etc.

Výměna poloh:
1 - 5, 2 - 6, 3 - 7 atd.

24.

25.

26.

27.

28.

29.

30.

31.

32.

Changes of position:
from 1st to 6th, 2nd to 7th and Thumb Positions.
Wechsel der Lagen:
1-6, 2-7 und Daumenaufsätze.

Changement des positions:
1-6, 2-7 et les positions du pouce.
Výměna poloh:
1-6, 2-7 a palcová poloha.

*) Bar introducing Thumb Position
*) Mesure introduisant la position du pouce
*) Der den Daumenaufsatz einführende Takt
*) Do palcové polohy uvádějící

B. & C? 18488

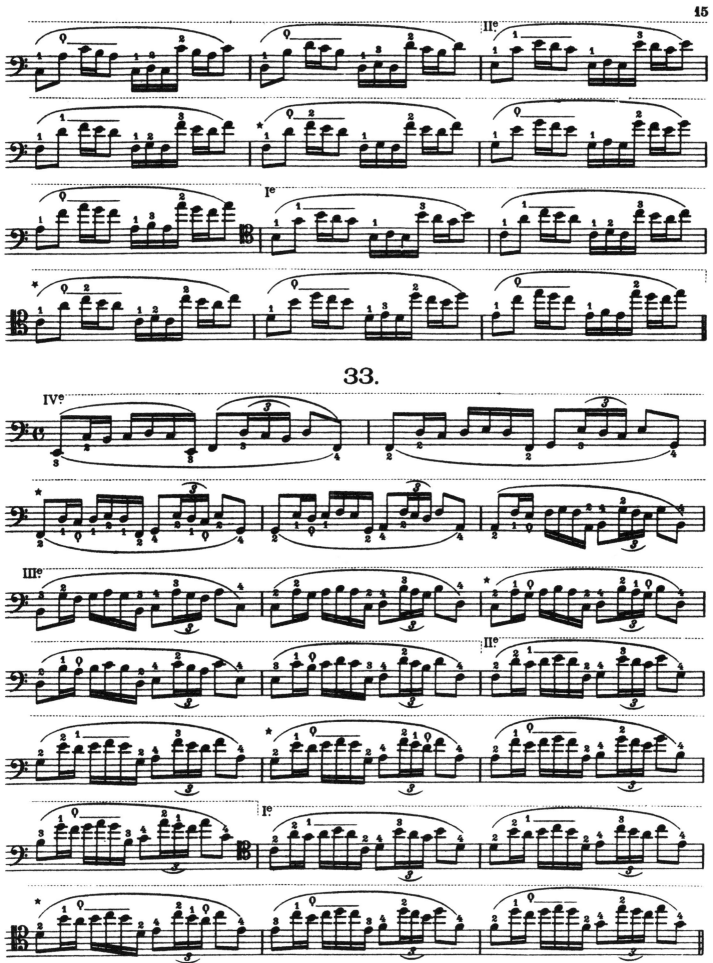

33.

34.

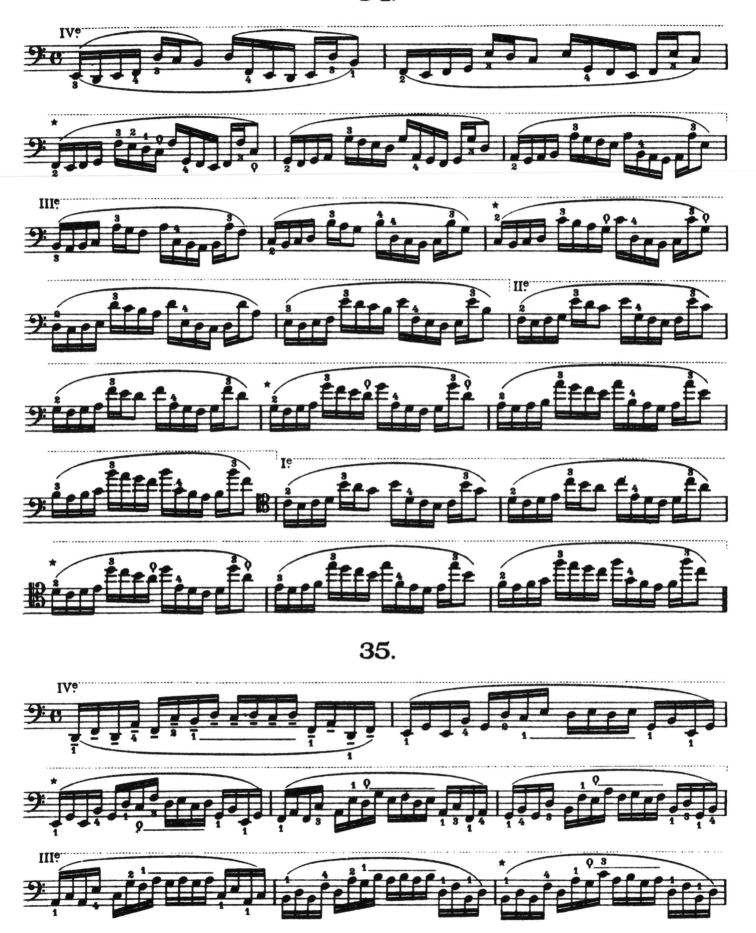

35.

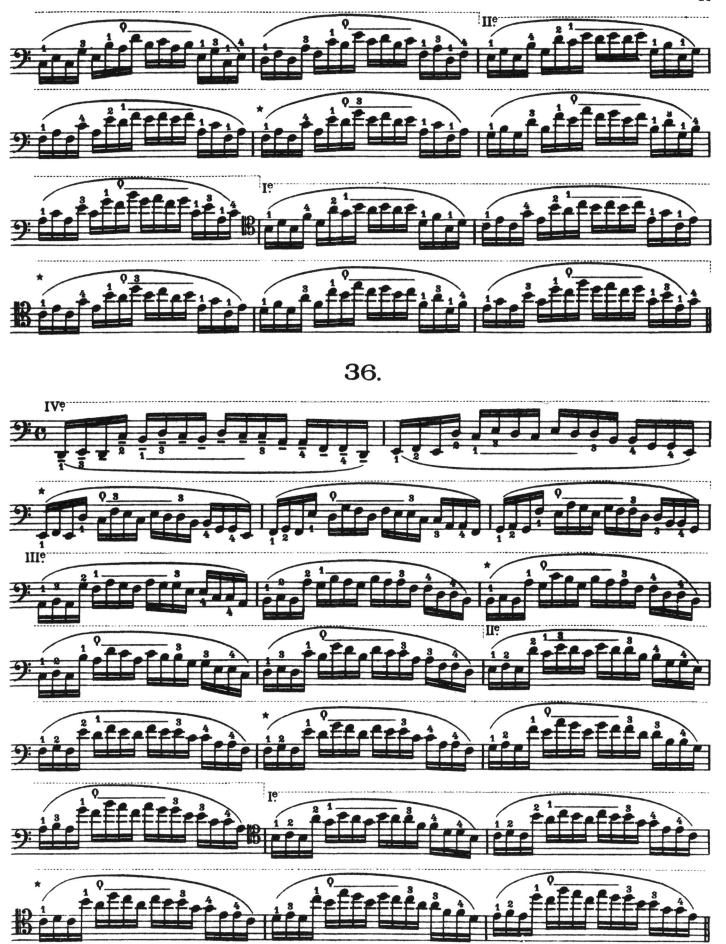

36.

37.

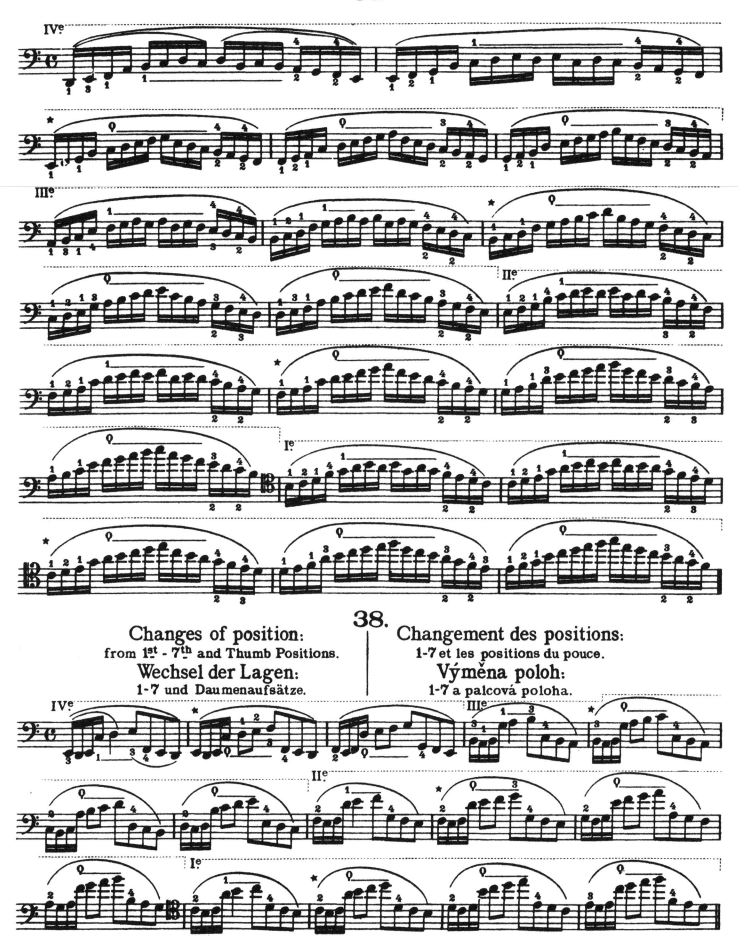

38.

Changes of position:
from 1st - 7th and Thumb Positions.

Wechsel der Lagen:
1-7 und Daumenaufsätze.

Changement des positions:
1-7 et les positions du pouce.

Výměna poloh:
1-7 a palcová poloha.

39.

40.

41.

42.

43.

44.

45.

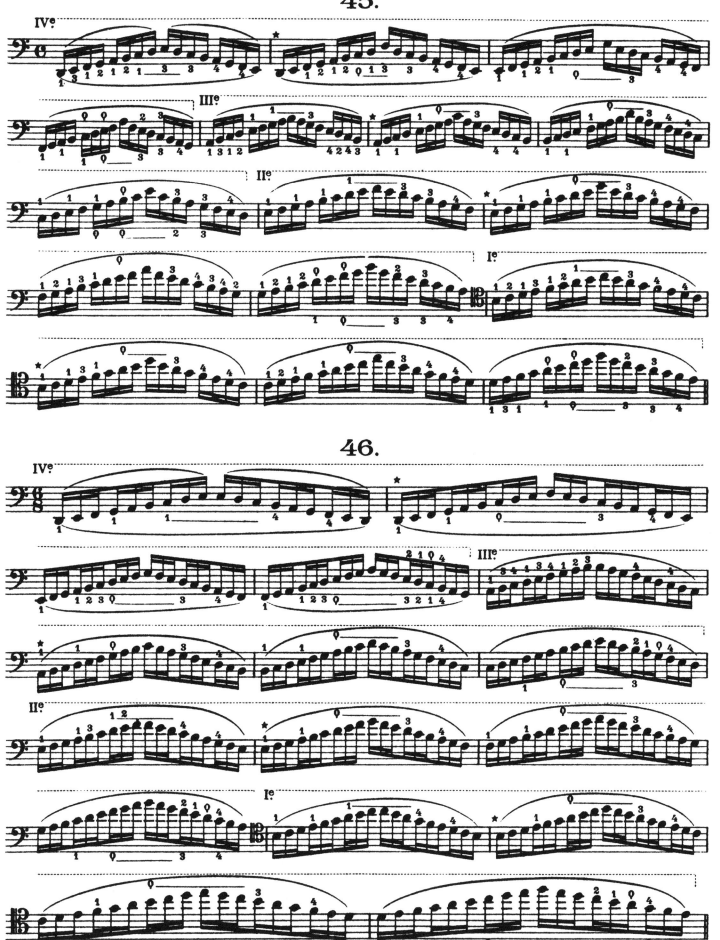

46.

47.

Changes of position:	**Changement des positions:**
1st to Thumb Position.	1- position du pouce.
Wechsel der Lagen:	**Výměna poloh:**
1- Daumenaufsatz.	1- palcová poloha.

48.

49.

50.

51.

52.

53.

54.

55.

56.

57.

Scales throughout 3 Octaves. | Gammes de 3 Octaves.

Tonleitern durch 3 Octaven. | Stupnice v rozsahu 3 Oktav.

C major
C dur. — Ut majeur

58.

59.

Printed and bound in Great Britain by
Caligraving Limited Thetford Norfolk